★NSYNC

"No Strings Attached"

TRIUMPH
BOOKS

CHICAGO

THE MARK OF THE QUAD CITIES

'N SYNC

*NSYNC IS
"No Strings Attached" boosts

*N CHARGE

the guys to the top of pop music

The five young men who make up one of the pop music world's biggest acts, *NSync, will not take a back seat to Backstreet Boys or any other group that impedes their path to pop dominance. *NSync's latest single, "Bye, Bye, Bye," was released to radio on Jan. 12, 2000 and became the most-added track at more than 200 contemporary hit radio stations. That broke the previous record of 145 additions held by the Backstreet Boys' first single off "Millennium," "I Want It That Way."

"Bye, Bye, Bye," which was not released to stores as a CD single, is from *NSync's highly anticipated sophomore CD, "No Strings Attached," scheduled to hit shelves throughout North America on March 21.

Although they have long since established themselves as world-class talents, *NSync members tend to bristle – quite understandably – when they are compared to the Backstreet Boys.

Group member Joey Fatone is quick to point out the differences.

"We try to have a Boyz II Men, Take 6 kind of feel," he said. "People tend to think (groups) all do one thing. Our harmonies are very soulful. That's out of the ordinary, first of all, then you put in these Take 6 harmonies, and not a lot of people are doing that. So while some groups would do a similar thing, we try to do it with a jazz feel."

According to 19-year-old Justin Timberlake, *NSync had more creative freedom while making their second album than when recording their self-titled debut album.

"It's definitely nice to have some creative freedom and to really express ourselves, but I think when you listen to the new album in comparison to our debut album, you'll say to yourself that

we took our sound to the next level," said Justin.

Twenty-one-year-old Lance Bass, the bass singer in the group, added, "No Strings Attached" is more personal and is a bit more edgy.

"It's more our style. We feel like this is our first album because we actually independently did this one."

Putting On Mouse Ears

Witnessing *NSync's leap to stardom, it may seem like the five guys settled easily into success. But while

*NSync may be calling the shots now, that wasn't always the case.

Comprised of band members from all across the United States, just like the Backstreet Boys, *NSync came together as a group in Orlando, Fla.

Fittingly for a band from Orlando, some of the group's members can trace their professional origins to the land of Mickey Mouse; more specifically, the Disney Channel's now defunct "Mickey Mouse Club" television show. That's where Joshua "JC" Chasez and Justin worked for nearly three years, and ☞

*NSYNC JUST HANGING AROUND WITH FANS!

*NSYNC

although they are five years apart in age, they quickly became friends. It's also where they met future pop music princesses Britney Spears and Christina Aguilera, and actress Keri Russell from WB's "Felicity."

After the "Mickey Mouse Club" was canceled, JC and Justin headed for Nashville, where they shared a vocal coach while working on solo projects. The two also took dance lessons from a choreographer who had previously worked with Michael Jackson and The Artist Formerly Known As Prince.

JC and Justin returned to Orlando, where they met Pittsburgh native Chris Kirkpatrick. Chris was working at Universal Studios as a "doo-wop" singer, and it was he who had the initial plans to put together a band. His dream of translating five-part harmonies into pop-music gold grew closer to reality when the trio met Joey Fatone of Brooklyn, N.Y.

The four young musicians came together and worked the Orlando-area club scene and wowed the mostly young female audiences with their slick moves and smooth song style. Their impromptu appearances started a buzz around town, inspiring the quartet to form a group. Lacking a bass-range voice, Justin's vocal coach in Memphis tracked down a young, blond-haired, green-eyed crooner aptly named Lance Bass from Clinton, Miss. Now with a complete group, the guys expanded their performances to theme parks, coffeehouses and discos.

The Birth Of *NSync

In August 1995, with the pieces all in place, the group was ready to discover stardom. However, there was still one glaring problem: The group didn't have a name. The boys brain-

stormed in vain for weeks trying to come up with possibilities, but it was Justin's mom who had an interesting idea. Commenting on how "in sync" the boys performed together, she suggested "*NSync," deriving the name from the spelling of each boy's names, using their last letters in their first names: Justin (N), Chris (S), Joey (Y), Lansten – the nickname for Lance (N) and JC (C).

The group's diversity is perhaps its greatest strength, and each member makes his own contribution to the now-popular *NSync sound.

Each member cites varying influences in his musical career, from Joey's love of rock 'n' roll groups such as Frankie Lyman and the Teenagers and The Temptations to Lance's prefer-ence for Garth Brooks and country sounds to Justin's inspiration of Stevie Wonder's soul-blended styles mixed with a little hip-hop energy.

Chris described *NSync's sound as "purely original. It's pop with an R&B twist. We take a lot of up-tempo songs and put harmonies behind them."

With the help of a former "Mickey

Mouse Club" cameraman, the boys made a promotional video. Their first attempt at a video was "rough," according to Chris. "We did it at the last minute, but it was all done by us – the printing of the posters, the choosing of the outfits, the song order, the choreography – everything. It was a lot of work for everyone."

In 1996, the video caught the attention of noted music impresario Lou Pearlman and his partner, Johnny Wright, who made New Kids on the Block a rage, and who, ironically, also managed the Backstreet Boys. Pearlman and Wright signed the group to a management contract.

Comparisons between *NSync and Backstreet Boys seemed inevitable, especially once people heard of both band's No. 1 commonality – the groups' management. However, *NSync members adamantly contend they're not out to copy anyone, much less Backstreet Boys.

"When we put our group together – and we were together six months before we met Johnny – I didn't even know who the Backstreet Boys were," said Justin.

Still, industry experts say the success of the Backstreet Boys opened the door to similarly composed groups such as *NSync.

"The Backstreet Boys paved the way and made people, including MTV, pay attention to this style of music and these types of groups," said Lewis Largent, MTV's vice president of music. "With their success, record companies went out and tried to sign more bands like them."

Overseas Success

By late 1997, the quintet and its management team convinced ☞

RCA Records to sign them to a contract. Sensing the market was ripe for a group to compete with Backstreet Boys, the guys enlisted the help of several well-established music industry producers, including Kristian Lundin, who had once worked with Backstreet Boys, and the late Denniz Pop, whose clients included artists such as Robyn and Ace of Base.

*NSync hit the studio to record a set of pop songs aimed at the teen market. To capitalize on the boy-band fervor in Europe (at that time, industry experts believed grunge still ruled in the U.S.), *NSync's handlers marketed their self-titled debut album exclusively in Europe, a strategy that had worked perfectly for Backstreet Boys.

"The pop music market here wasn't happening then," said Joey. "Hanson and the Spice Girls helped open that door."

The fab five headed to Europe and played to packed houses and frenzied audiences (mostly young girls) in Germany and the Netherlands. The single "I Want You Back" became a smash hit overseas, and the group broke long-standing European sales records. A sold-out tour followed, bringing the boys in front of screaming fans in multiple countries and across several continents, virtually everywhere around the world with the notable exclusion of the United States. With the success of its first tour assured, *NSync began laying the groundwork for its next challenge. It was time for the group to return home and transfer its growing popularity.

"I think the hardest thing is being so big over in Europe and then coming home and nobody having a clue," said Chris in a past interview.

"Because this is our home and

FROM TOP: LISA ROSE / GLOBE; SONIA MOSKOWITZ / GLOBE; MARK ALLAN / GLOBE

*NSYNC IS HUGE IN THE UNITED STATES NOW, BUT SEVERAL YEARS AGO THE GROUP GOT ITS BIG BREAK IN EUROPE.

THE GUYS IN *NSYNC PRIDE THEMSELVES ON STAGING ENERGETIC LIVE SHOWS, COMPLETE WITH UNIQUE ENTRANCE MUSIC AND COSTUMES AND HIGH-FLYING TUNES LIKE "SAILING."

America is the No. 1 market, it's a major thing to succeed here," added Lance. "But if we don't succeed, we always have the rest of our work. ... We just have high hopes that we're going to do great over here."

Lance's hopeful prediction would soon come true.

The Next Big Thing

In the spring of 1998, *NSync's self-titled CD was released in America. Its climb up the charts was nothing less than meteoric. The group took off after a Disney Channel special in the early fall of that year (an opportunity Backstreet Boys had incidentally turned down) and some heavy exposure on MTV. Two singles from the CD, "I Want You Back" and "Tearin' Up My Heart," became top 40 hits and boosted the album to platinum status within four months of its release.

The boys were on their way. Teen magazines such as "Tiger Beat" and "Girls' Life" called *NSync "the next big thing." *NSync started out on a small-venue tour, playing places like Chicago's House of Blues and even small county fairs in downstate Wisconsin. After that swing, however, *NSync found itself on the much bigger "Ain't No Stoppin' Us Now" tour, opening for Janet Jackson's "Velvet Rope" tour and singing the national anthem at Orlando Magic basketball and Philadelphia Phillies baseball games. They also performed at the Miss Teen USA pageant and made guest appearances on "The Tonight Show" and "Live! With Regis &

Kathie Lee."

After the success of *NSync's debut album, RCA quickly sent the group back to the studio to record a Christmas CD.

"Not just anybody can put out a Christmas album," said JC. "(You) have to have somewhat of a following for people to want to pick it up. And that made us feel very good."

Through their sudden stardom, the guys' tight friendships on and off the stage have been unaffected. Before every performance, the boys prepare themselves with their own pre-show ritual. First, a quick game of hackey sack, then the group, their musicians and the entire entourage – including security and wardrobe teams – join hands in a circle to recite a prayer. One final group hug and it's showtime!

Out Of Sync

In 1999, *NSync made more than just music when it became embroiled in a yearlong lawsuit with its record label over contract agreements. The boys alleged they had been exploited and betrayed, and their opponents insisted that the boys were "ungrateful and greedy, arrogantly walking away from a binding contract."

"Rolling Stone" called the legal battle one of "the music industry's nastiest legal skirmishes in years." The court case pitted *NSync and Jive against the group's former business partners TransContinental Records (led by Lou Pearlman) and its larger worldwide partner BMG (owner of RCA Records). As one of the lawyers involved in the case summed up, "This case is about nothing, nothing but money." ☞

In late December, *NSync announced an out-of-court settlement with its old record company that enabled them to join the red-hot Jive label, which also boasts pop stars Backstreet Boys and Britney Spears.

The Right Stuff

Despite the natural comparisons with Backstreet Boys, the members of *NSync are determined to carve out a unique voice for themselves. So far it appears that there are more than enough dedicated fans to keep both groups riding high on the charts for a long time.

Although the two have crossed paths on several occasions – including at a celebrity basketball game in Germany a couple years ago – both groups remain friendly rivals.

"It's not like we want to compete with one or two bands," said Justin. "We put the group together ourselves. I think that's something that's paid off in the long run because we were friends before we got a management team and before we got a record deal."

Lance added, "Everything that we do is always together, and I think that's what makes the group unique."

Regardless of future success or failure, *NSync's members maintain a bond that will endure.

"There's nothing better than going out with your friends and having a good time," said JC. "And that's what it is. These guys are my best friends, and we get to go out and we get to see each other have fun. That's the best part about the job."

Joey agreed. "Success is the test if our friendship keeps on. And if it does, perfect. We actually don't want to be without the others." *NSYNC*

LISA ROSE / GLOBE (2); BERNHARD KUHMSTEDT / RETNA (2)

*NSYNC'S MEMBERS APPRECIATE THE FACT THAT THEY ALL STILL GET ALONG AND FEEL LIKE ONE BIG FAMILY.

*NSYNC

The Making of
'No Strings Attached'

*Nsync busts out with a killer new album

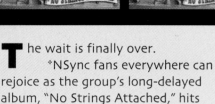

The wait is finally over. *NSync fans everywhere can rejoice as the group's long-delayed album, "No Strings Attached," hits shelves on March 21.

The guys of *NSync – Lance Bass, JC Chasez, Joey Fatone, Chris Kirkpatrick and Justin Timberlake – are thrilled that their follow-up effort on Jive Records is ready for release.

"This album is a step above the first one," said Joey. "We experienced a lot of things since the first album came out. We've grown up a little bit more. Hopefully, we'll evolve with the fans and evolve with the music.

"We're adding different beats, different sounds, just to make it a little more edgier. But, it's still gonna have *NSync harmonies and sound."

"We made sure that whatever happens, we keep creative control," said Chris of making the new CD. "We keep creative control and we keep control of our own destinies."

Lance agrees that "No Strings Attached" carries a bit more creative bite than the boys have been used to. He also promises that it will have more of a personal feel for fans because each member of the group had more control in the recording process.

"It's a little bit more edgy," said Lance. "It's more our style. We feel like this is like our first album because we actually independently did this one."

JC added, "The new album has a slightly different sound, more of an R&B edge, and more uptempo. We're just taking pop music to another level."

So, what's on the album, you ask? "No Strings Attached" includes songs from Kristian Lundin and Jake Schulze ("Bye, Bye, Bye," the first single); Max Martin, Rami and Andreas Carlsson ("It's

Gonna Be Me"); Richard Marx ("This I Promise You"); Guy Roche and Diane Warren ("That's When I'll Stop Loving You"); Teddy Reilly (a cover of Johnny Kemp's '80s hit "Just Got Paid"); and She'kspere ("Makes Me Ill").

The album also includes two songs co-written and co-produced by JC ("Space Cowboy" and "Digital Get Down") and one co-written and co-produced by Justin ("Good For You"). Justin describes "Good For You" as a glimpse into his love style.

"It's about how I would treat a girl if I was in love with her," said Justin. "Like, 'I know the way I am is a bit overwhelming, but I want you to know that it's all from the heart.' "

JC said he was thrilled that TLC's Lisa "Left Eye" Lopes raps on "Space Cowboy" because it adds a female dimension to *NSync's music.

"When we did the song, we actually just put a dance break in it, and she's been doing all kinds of collaborations," said JC. "And she comes across really cool. I think it's cool to have a female's perspective on a male album. As far as female rappers, she was the choice right away."

The first single from the new album, "Bye, Bye, Bye," is already a huge success. The video for the song is consistently No. 1 on MTV's "Total Request Live," and promotional CDs for the hot song (which was not released in stores) are selling for big bucks at online auction sites like eBay.com.

Getting back in the studio to record new material was refreshing for everyone in the group.

"We were given total control in the studio," said Joey about making the new CD. "We chose the songwriters and producers we wanted to work with. With this album, we are being completely true to ourselves."

"I'm happiest in the studio," added JC.

"Don't get me wrong. I love doing shows, but I love creating the stuff that people are going to hear over and over again."

The name "No Strings Attached" has a lot of meaning for the group as well, especially in light of legal issues that prompted *NSync to leave RCA Records for Jive.

"It has different meanings," said Lance. " 'No Strings Attached' is usually said when they want you to check out something. We said it 'cause we want you to listen to it, and you decide what to think, have your own personal opinion. And we also feel finally free of what has been holding us back, we are in control of everything we do. Groups like us are usually all guided about and told what to do, and that is so not us. So were are here to tell you we have no strings attached."

So, what's next? Get ready fans, because *NSync is going to be "in your face" for the rest of 2000 and beyond.

On March 20, the day before the new album is slated to be released, *NSync is scheduled to do a live radio interview on the syndicated AMFM, as well as play tracks from "No Strings Attached."

Fans also should fire up their VCRs to tape all of *NSync's appearances to promote the album. Jive Records said *NSync was scheduled to appear again on "Total Request Live" (March 7 and 21) and "Ultra Sound" (March 18).

In addition, the following *NSync appearances are confirmed: "Saturday Night Live" (March 11); "Good Morning America" (March 13); "The Rosie O'Donnell Show" (March 20); Nickelodeon's "All That" (March 25); "The View" (March 27); and "The Tonight Show with Jay Leno" (April 4).

In stores, you can expect to find the new album showcased in special lit-up displays. Wal-Mart will even air a special broadcast in all of its stores on March 21.

"No Strings Attached" is definitely expected to be one of the biggest sellers of 2000. And let's not forget *NSync's huge North American summer tour, scheduled to begin in May.

"We're going to do whatever it takes for us to get our music to the fans," said JC. *NSYNC

JC

JOEY

JUSTIN

LANCE

CHRIS

*NSYNC

PINUPS

JUSTIN

JUSTIN

JC

JC

MELANIE EDWARDS / RETNA

*NSYNC PINUPS

JOEY

JOEY

CHRIS

CHRIS

LANCE

LANCE

MELANIE EDWARDS / RETNA

*NSYNC
PERSONAL

PROFILES

James Lance Bass

Birthdate: May 4, 1979
Sign: Taurus
Birthplace: Clinton, Miss.
Height: 5 feet 11 inches
Nicknames: PooFoo, Lansten, Scoop
Fave food: French toast
Fave ice cream flavor: butter pecan
Fave movies: "Clue," "Armageddon"
Fave musicians: Garth Brooks, Boyz II Men, Brian McKnight
Fave colors: Red and blue
Fave TV show: "I Love Lucy"
Fave holiday: Christmas
Scared of: Things that buzz (like bugs!)
Childhood ambition: To be an astronaut
Hobbies: Jet-skiing
Bad habit: Biting his nails
Collects: Tasmanian Devil stuff, Dr. Seuss artwork, antique knives and guns
Prized possession: His American Music Award and a 20th anniversary bracelet from legendary rap group Sugarhill Gang

THE PERFECT GENTLEMAN

Lance might have been the last guy to become a member of *NSync, but this sincerely sweet Southern gentleman is definitely No. 1 when it comes to charming everyone he meets. His ideal date is dinner at home (he insists on cooking it from scratch!), followed by a movie. "I definitely like things simple," he explained. "I like an innocent-type girl, not a total goody-goody, but nice, someone who can baby me. I like a religious girl. Someone who keeps herself up and knows how to have a good time. And she has to be able to take a joke."

Lance loves it when he can get his friends and family together for a barbecue where all the food is homemade – hand-mixed hamburger patties, green bean casserole, potato salad and his own specialty, Chocolate Dream Pie.

Lance recently built his first home in his native Mississippi and created a man-made lake behind his place so he can jet-ski whenever he has a chance. The group's been so busy that he's barely been able to stay there, but he can't wait to get back. "Every room is different. I especially love this one room that has a Dr. Seuss theme," he said. "It's all reds and blues, and I have original Dr. Seuss artwork in there."

COUNTRY BOY

"The first time I knew that I wanted to be on stage was when I saw Garth Brooks in concert. I was 14. I thought his show was incredible. I thought, 'That's what I want to do,'" said Lance. Lance loves country music more than most people realize. When *NSync got to perform with Alabama at last year's Country Music Awards, Lance called it a dream come true. Even though he's a world-famous celebrity himself, Lance admits he was super-nervous backstage where he met country stars like Dolly Parton and Shania Twain. "It was so cool!" he said.

BUSINESS-MINDED BABE

Lance isn't known as the most business-minded member of *NSync for nothing. He's a budding music manager whose love of music and helping others led him to form his own company, FreeLance Entertainment. FreeLance handles the careers of two up-and-coming, country-pop artists: Meredith Edwards and Jack Defoe. "Meredith is amazing," gushed Lance. "She's going to be the next LeAnn Rimes."

SIMPLY HEAVEN-LY

Acting has always been a dream for Lance, and now it's a dream come true! He recently made his small-screen debut on the hit WB show "7th Heaven," where he played actress Beverley Mitchell's new boyfriend. Lance got the acting gig because Beverley is a huge fan and suggested the idea to the TV show's producers.

"I was nervous," he said. "It's a lot harder than people think, with 50 people watching you and cameras everywhere. And I really have to lose the southern accent. I'm supposed to be playing an Italian Californian!"

Lance will again get to act up – along with all the other members of *NSync – when the group starts filming its first movie later this year. "We've been talking to Tom Hanks' production company about it for a year now," said Lance. "It's going to be a real movie – we won't be playing ourselves; it won't be like the Spice Girls movie."

Joshua Scott "JC" Chasez

Birthdate: August 8, 1976
Sign: Leo
Birthplace: Washington, D.C.
Height: 5 feet 11 inches
Nicknames: Shazzam, Big Daddy, Sleepy
Fave food: Chinese
Fave ice cream flavor: Mint chocolate chip
Fave movies: The "Star Wars" and "Indiana Jones" series
Fave musicians: Sting, Seal, Stevie Wonder
Fave color: Blue
Fave holiday: Christmas
Fave theme-park ride: Tower of Terror at Walt Disney World
Fave team: Washington Redskins football
Childhood ambition: To be an engineer, architect or carpenter
Bad habit: Bites his nails
Scared of: Needles
Collects: Hard Rock Cafe menus

MAKING IT HAPPEN

Ambition? Check. Dedication? Check. Commitment? You betcha. JC is by far the most music-career-minded member of *NSync. He writes songs for *NSync (he carries a microcassette recorder with him everywhere) and is even taking on writing duties for other groups! He's producing a few tracks on Wild Orchid's upcoming CD and even penned a couple of the gorgeous threesome's songs, including the track "Fire." JC admitted he's "always been a workaholic. Once I go into something, I dive in with both feet." JC said he's also the serious one. "Everybody's got their job. My job is to remind people to be on time. I'm the serious one, and I like to make sure that everything runs smooth. I'm the guy who gets everybody to buckle down."

MOUSE MUSIC

After his mom spotted an ad for Mickey Mouse Club auditions, JC figured he would take a chance. After all, he had nothing to lose. "I just went to the audition for the heck of it," he recalled. "I didn't think I had a chance because I had never done anything like it before. It was my first audition, but sure enough, I scored it. I got pretty lucky." We bet talent had more to do with it than luck. JC starred for four years on the Disney show, where he met fellow Mouseketeer Justin, as well as pop stars Britney Spears, Christina Aguilera and actress Keri Russell. "The friends I made on that show are lifetime friends. My fondest memories were hanging out at the beach, hanging at the apartment with my buddies and co-stars," said JC.

OUT OF THIS WORLD

There's one thing JC won't live without: His Leo necklace. "I've only taken it off once in the last, like, five years, and that was only for a few hours," he said. "It was so weird. I won't take it off for anything now." He's fascinated by astrology and recently received a book on astro stuff that he takes everywhere. "It tells you all about your sign, but it gets even deeper than that – into moon signs, sun signs, Chinese astrology, everything," he said. "It's eerie how revealing that stuff is. It helps you learn a lot about yourself."

COLLECTING CUTIE

Lucky for JC that his group travels all over the world, because it makes it easier for him to add to his eclectic collection of Hard Rock Cafe menus. He has more than 30, and among his most prized additions are menus from Paris and London. Then there's his favorite Hard Rock item: "A pin of a menu that I snagged in London. A lady was waiting on me and she was wearing a pin of a menu. There's only 15 to 20 given out every year. And it's only for employees who do exceptional work around the world." She was so charmed by JC and his collecting habits that she got permission from her boss and gave up her pin!

Joshua Scott "JC" Chasez - *NSYNC Personal Profile

BERNHARD KUHMSTEDT / RETNA

*NSYNC 37

Joseph Anthony Fatone, Jr.

Birthdate: January 28, 1977
Sign: Aquarius
Birthplace: Brooklyn, N.Y.
Height: 6 feet
Nicknames: Flirt, Phat One, Superman
Fave food: Italian
Fave ice cream flavor: Mint chocolate chip
Fave movie: "Willy Wonka and the Chocolate Factory"
Fave musicians: Doo-wop groups (like Frankie Lymon and the Teenagers),
Boyz II Men, Mariah Carey, Stevie Wonder
Fave colors: Purple and red
Fave TV show: "South Park"
Fave holiday: Christmas
Fave theme-park ride: Tower of Terror at Walt Disney World
Bad habit: Bites his nails
Scared of: Commitment
Collects: Superman memorabilia

FLIRT ALERT

There's no question about it: Perpetual prankster Joey is by far the most flirtatious, fun-loving member of *NSync. Just take it from his mom: "He's a party kid, likes his girls, flirting since he was in kindergarten," she said. "He hasn't changed at all." Joey said his friends would describe him as "always being up for a good time." Equally charming and goofy, this native New Yorker is a pure partier. "I like to go out to clubs, check it out, see what's going on," he said. "One day, me, Lance and Justin may open up a club."

A flirting fanatic, Joey prefers a straight-up approach, girls who aren't afraid to speak their mind. "Not necessarily aggressive, but someone who will come right up and start talking to me." This single guy doesn't have as much time for dating as he would like, but that's OK by him. "We're so busy, and we're never in one place for very long, so I don't think I could be a good boyfriend to someone right now," he said. "You've gotta keep your options open. I let girls know what's up."

NO PAIN, NO GAIN

He's all about smooth moves nowadays, but as a kid, Joey was the world's biggest klutz! He used to wear a cape and "fly" through the house showing off, pretending he was Superman. "The emergency room staff knew him by his first name," said his father. Before he was 5, Joey had gotten 12 stitches and 18 cuts closed with butterfly bandages, but his love of performing was born.

ACTING UP

Music is his mission right now, but Joey's ultimate love is acting. As a child, his dad ran a theater group, and as a teenager Joey performed in musicals and Shakespearean and one-act plays in Orlando, Fla. (he moved there from Brooklyn when he was 13). Joey admits he hopes to turn leading man and take the silver screen by storm someday (he had small roles in two movies as a kid: "Once Upon A Time In America" and "Matinee"). "I love acting. I grew up doing theater," he said. "I want to do movies – drama, comedy, everything. I love a challenge." But if someone made a movie about the lives of the members of *NSync, Joey wouldn't want to play himself. "Ryan Phillippe would play Justin. I think Ross from 'Friends' would play me, Chris? Adam Sandler. JC?

Probably somebody like Luke Perry or something. Lance? Uh, I'll get back to you on that one."

HERO WORSHIP

It's a bird! It's a plane! It's Joey's crazy collection of tons and tons of Superman stuff. Before he joined *NSync, he "was collecting [Superman] T-shirts and hats and stuff. One day I wore it for a photo shoot. I guess that's how I got the nickname," he explained. You can usually catch Joey wearing his diamond-and-gold necklace in the shape of the Superman "S" logo and his ruby-and-diamond Superman earrings. "I like the symbol," said Joey. "I think it's cool." A fan once knitted a sweater for him with the "S" logo on front. "It took her two months to make it," Joey said with genuine appreciation.

When Joey met Christopher Reeve, who played the caped one in the Superman movies, at a New Jersey *NSync concert, "I just stood there and said, 'Hi,'– I didn't say much. I was very, very happy. His wife wrote an autograph to me, because she's authorized to sign his signature [Reeve is paralyzed], and wrote, 'To one fan from another.' It was a really great feeling."

Joseph Anthony Fatone, Jr. - *NSYNC Personal Profile

Christopher Alan Kirkpatrick

BOB BERG / RETNA

Birthdate: October 17, 1971

Sign: Libra

Birthplace: Clarion, Pa.

Height: 5 feet 9 inches

Nicknames: Crazy, Psycho, Puerto Rico

Fave food: Tacos

Fave TV shows: "The Simpsons," "South Park"

Fave musicians: Busta Rhymes, Beastie Boys, Indigo Girls, Counting Crows

Fave color: Silver

Fave theme-park ride: Alien Encounter at Walt Disney World

Fave team: Any team from Pittsburgh, Pa.

Fave holiday: Halloween

Scared of: Heights

Bad habit: Bites his nails

Collects: Records (he used to be a DJ)

Prized possession: Autographed photo of Bruce Lee

Childhood ambition: To be a psychologist

WILD AND CRAZY GUY

Chris definitely lives up to his reputation as the wild man of the group. His friends can't believe the stuff he pulls (like going surfing in the middle of a hurricane!), and Chris is more than happy to own up to it. "I'm the trouble, I'm the poison in the group, the troublemaker," he said. "Every day I'll do something and try to get the other guys to do it." But while he might like to live on the edge, Chris is also incredibly down-to-earth and compassionate, a free spirit who's always positive. After college, where he studied music and psychology, Chris took a big chance and moved to Orlando, where he landed a job as a 1950s doo-wop singer at Universal Studios. He'd been in singing groups before, "but this time I really wanted to take it seriously," he said. "So I called up a bunch of my buddies." The rest is history.

SEASONED PERFORMER

Chris is such a true talent that he's been belting out songs since he was a baby! His mom said it probably has a lot to do with the fact that everyone in his family is a musician — his great-grandparents were in bands, his grandma was trained as an opera singer, his grandpa made five country-western records and all his aunts and uncles are singers today. His mom even teaches voice lessons! Chris really learned to love performing when he landed the lead role in "Oliver!" in fifth grade. After that, he took up trombone, keyboard and guitar. He really expressed himself through his music and his wicked sense of humor, something his mom says she's grateful he had the opportunity to do. Because although Chris loves surfing, football and tons of other sports, he was always a small kid. "Tiny, almost elf-like," said his mother. "For him to survive being small and not get beat up every day, he became the funniest person in school."

GIVING BACK

"Somebody gave us a chance, and sometimes I feel like we just owe it to everyone else," said Chris of his philosophy on helping others out. He's talking about karma, and how he believes that what goes around comes around. It's part of the reason he's working with singer/songwriter Chris Irizarry, a good friend from his pre-*NSync days. "He plays guitar and sings. He's really, really great," said Chris, who's hoping to help Irizarry get a record deal.

BRANCHING OUT

Chris has always felt a need to create, so when he's not making music, he's busy overseeing FuMan Skeeto, his clothing, graphic design and music-production company. The clothing line is based around brightly colored T-shirts and sweatshirts that have a skater-kid appeal. Chris' girlfriend is in charge of manufacturing, and her roommate, actress Danielle Fishel (Lance's ex-girlfriend), is the line's spokesperson. Eventually, Chris hopes to make his FuMan Skeeto line available on the Web at www.fumanskeeto.com and in stores.

Justin Randall Timberlake

NICK TANGLEY / ALL ACTION

Birthdate: January 31, 1981

Sign: Aquarius

Birthplace: Memphis, Tenn.

Height: 6 feet

Nicknames: Shot, Bounce, Mr. Smooth

Fave foods: Cereal and pasta

Fave movies: "The Usual Suspects," "12 Monkeys"

Fave musicians: Brian McKnight, Take 6

Fave color: Baby blue

Fave theme-park ride: Space Mountain at Walt Disney World

Fave holiday: Christmas

Childhood ambition: To be a professional singer or basketball player

Scared of: Snakes, spiders and sharks

Bad habit: Burping

Collects: Sneakers, basketball stuff

SOULFUL SWEETIE

The youngest member of *NSync also happens to be one of the group's most sensitive guys, a true artist who takes everything to heart. He's also taking charge on *NSync's new album, "No Strings Attached," including writing the song "Good For You." "It's about how I would treat a woman if I was in love with her," explained Justin. "Like, 'I know the way I am is a bit overwhelming, but I want you to know that it's all from the heart.' That seems to be my problem with all my ex-girlfriends. I think I loved them too much from the very beginning. I found out girls need to chase a little." Justin is currently single but dating, and says he's happy with the situation. "A lot of girls have cheated on me in the past, so it's hard for me to trust. But once I fall, I fall hard."

KID CROONER

"I've pretty much always been in entertainment," said Justin. "I did 'The Mickey Mouse Club' for two years and before that I did 'Star Search' when I was 11. Before that I was singing in church. Although I never imagined something like this where we tour the world!"

Justin was one of only seven kids selected from more than 30,000 who auditioned for MMC. He and fellow cast member JC Chasez became fast friends on the set, where they built the foundation of what is today *NSync. Justin and JC also became buds with present-day pop peers Britney Spears and Christina Aguilera and "Felicity" star Keri Russell during their MMC days.

ALL IN THE FAMILY

All the guys' mothers are super-supportive of *NSync, but Justin's mom, Lynn Harless, really goes the extra mile. It was even her idea to call the group *NSync! The guys had been trying to come up with a name for weeks, but nothing seemed to fit. One day, Lynn said how "in sync" their harmonies and dance moves were. The name stuck. Even better? She then discovered how fitting the moniker really was. While playing with the letters, she realized that the last letters of all their first names spelled out *NSync. That's when Justin, Chris, Joey, Lansten (his nickname) and JC knew it was meant to be. Justin's mom also manages an all-girl group called Innosense (Britney Spears was supposed to be in it before she decided to go solo). The female fivesome's debut album will be out in the next few months on RCA Records, *NSync's old label.

MODEL BEHAVIOR

Viewers tuning into "The Wonderful World of Disney" which airs on Sunday nights on ABC, were in for a pleasant treat in a March made-for-TV movie, thanks to Justin. The newly brunette babe played a male model in "Janine and Alex: Cover Girls."

Speaking of model behavior, Justin is playing leading man in more ways than one: He's spearheading an effort to improve education in the arts in schools across the country through the Justin Timberlake Foundation. Its goal is to support fine arts in schools so that disciplines like drama, dance, music and the like will be available to every child no matter how rich or poor they may be. "I want to raise enough money to get things up to speed with technology and inspire kids to pursue music," explained Justin. "They should have everything they need to really do it."

Think you can read the *NSync guys' hearts and minds like an open book? Read on to get a little closer to your favorite *NSync man and get the scoop on what they're really thinking.

Q: Lisa "Left Eye" Lopes from TLC collaborated with you guys for a song on your new CD, "No Strings Attached." Who else would you like to work with?

Lance: "We've always wanted to do something with Shania Twain. I think that would be different – a country singer and a pop group. We've also always loved Jewel and Janet Jackson and, oh gosh, Lauryn Hill."

UP CLOSE
AND PERSONAL

Your five favorite guys discuss everything from love to making their new CD

*NSYNC 45

Chris: "I'd like to do a duet with Gwen Stefani [of No Doubt]. Only I wouldn't sing. I'd just be asking her on a date the whole time!"

Q: How do you think your new songs are different from your other material?

Justin: "We had more creative freedom this time. I think that when you listen to this album in comparison to our debut album, you'll say to yourself that we took our sound to the next level."

Lance: " 'No Strings Attached' is more personal than our first album. It's a little bit more edgy. It's more our style. We feel like this is like our first album because we independently did this one."

JC: "Every song was hand-picked by us. It's a very personal album."

Q: We know you love cartoons – what's your fave?

Chris: "I like cartoons in general. Of course, I love 'The Simpsons' and 'South Park,' and I'm a huge 'Spider-Man' fan."

JC: " 'Ren and Stimpy' and 'South Park.' When I was younger, I liked 'Thundercats' and 'Superfriends.' "

Q: Who's your favorite "South Park" character?

Chris: "Cartman! We've each got 'South Park' characters – Joey is Kenny, Justin is Mr. Mackey, JC is Stan, Lance is Mr. Hanky, and I'm Eric Cartman."

Q: What's the best prank you've ever pulled on someone else in *NSync?

Chris: "There have been a lot of pranks. But one time, when JC feel asleep on a plane, I took all sorts of stuff from the plane and put it all over his head and everywhere. Then I took pictures of him and I had never told him about it until I showed him the pictures later."

Joey: "One time Lance was sleeping and I put whipped cream on his head. He wasn't too happy,

but it was definitely funny to all the guys."

Lance: "I fell asleep in the dressing room, and Joey put whipped cream and Beanie Babies® all over my head. It's on tape! I got him back though. I just took the whipped cream and put it on his hair – we had a war."

Q: What's your most endearing quality?

Chris: "Probably my loyalty and honesty."

JC: "My sincerity."

Q: What do you think of girls with pierced tongues?

Chris: "Whatever cranks their boat. They don't bother me."

Joey: "I was thinking about getting my tongue pieced for a while. I actually pierced my eyebrow, but it rejected it. I don't know about the tongue – it might affect my singing."

Q: Boxers or briefs?

Everyone: "Boxer briefs!"

Q: What was you first kiss like?

Justin: "I was nervous. And I was with my girlfriend at the time, in sixth grade. I was infatuated."

Chris: "It was awkward because we were playing Kiss Tag, so after she kissed me, she punched me. I had to learn at a very young age that women are nothing but trouble. Just kidding!"

Joey: "I was pushed into the closet like in the old movies. We didn't know how to kiss. We just used our mouths. I didn't know what I was doing. I was sweating and nervous!"

Lance: "I was 5 years old. I don't remember what it was like; it was just a peck. We had a homecoming game, and we were the little prince and princess of the game. We had to carry a crown and scepter, and they made us kiss."

Q: What's the most romantic thing that you've ever done for a girl?

Justin: "I cooked someone dinner, and she later cheated on me. I made pasta Alfredo with crab meat. That's the most romantic thing I've ever done."

Joey: "It wasn't the most romantic thing, but me and my friend took these girls – they always wanted to have a picnic – so we bought Kentucky Fried Chicken, and we all went to a park and we set it up and everything. It was a surprise we gave them. It was kind of cool."

JC: "I'm pathetic. I'm not so romantic, I'm such a chicken. I think I'm just a little shy when it comes to that stuff. I don't do a lot of flowers and candy because, of course, it's too clichéd. But the problem is, it's always a nice sentiment, no matter what. It's better to at least do that than do nothing. I mean, the best thing I can do is give somebody a really nice compliment or take them somewhere nice."

Lance: "I've never, like, sung to anybody or stuff like that. I like formal things. I love going out to nice dinners. I love dressing up. I like cooking people dinner. And we'd have a real formal-type dinner at her house or something like that, a candlelight dinner."

Q: Do you believe in love at first sight?

Chris: "I believe in the idea of love at first sight. I don't think you can fall in love with someone if you don't know her, but I believe you can have a connection that turns into love. I want a girl who can have fun doing whatever, wherever – someone who doesn't need material things to make her happy. A free spirit, that's the type of person I like."

Justin: "Hopefully, when I meet 'The One,' I'll know it's her and that it's meant to be. I like a girl who's confident, with a sense of humor, a good listener, somebody with a sensitive heart. I am a hopeless romantic, and I don't get off on people who make fun of other people. Somebody I could learn from, who would complement me, who could help me grow as a person."

JC: "I don't worry about that. I like a girl who maintains herself but isn't arrogant, who is understanding and makes me laugh."

Q: Who would your celebrity dream date be?

love the guys and they don't get on my nerves. We have a lot of fun together."

Q: If you could change one thing about yourself, what would it be?

Chris: "Probably my height. I'd want to be taller."

Q: What's your favorite place to go on tour?

Chris: "I liked South Africa a lot, because of the mountains right on the water, and we saw seals and sharks. That was just amazing. Plus I got to surf!"

Joey: "South Africa was a great trip. Asia. All around the U.S. Every place has a different thing that I remember. In Germany, the architecture was great. And a lot of places in New York City have some good memories."

Lance: "Liechtenstein because it was the most peaceful country you'll ever go to."

Q: Do you guys have any interesting rituals before you go on stage?

Joey: "We warm up our vocal chords and our bodies. And then we pray."

Lance: "We have about an hour before every concert where we relax. Our wardrobe assistants are licensed masseuses, so we get massages, and that relaxes us." ***NSYNC***

Joey: "Hmmm ... maybe Sandra Bullock, or Janet Jackson. It's a toss-up."

JC: "Salma Hayek, and there's a girl from a movie, 'She's All That,' Rachael Leigh Cook. There's something cute about her that I dig, and I don't dig a lot of actresses."

Q: What's the weirdest thing you've ever autographed?

Chris: "Undergarments. That's really embarrassing, too."

Q: What's the weirdest thing a fan has done to meet you?

JC: "We've seen it all. People have snuck in the luggage racks, tried to hide themselves in our hotel rooms..."

Lance: "Well, there was a strange thing someone did at a concert: We were in Europe and doing our first tour ever. I was down very close to the front row, and one of the girls down there just threw water in my face. I saw her later, and she was crying because she thought she had hurt me or something."

Q: What's your biggest pet peeve about all the other guys?

Justin: Joey is dirty, in more ways than one. Chris is really hyper, but that's not really a pet peeve – he's funny when he's hyper. JC is quite serious and he always comes into a conversation in the middle and asks a question that was asked five minutes ago. He does that every time! And Lance? When we play hackey sack before we go on stage, Lance is a little too serious about it. But seriously, I

Before They

How the men of *NSync got

Were Stars

their start

With millions of adoring fans around the world, a handful of chart-topping CDs and enough awards to fill a tour bus, you might think "Easy Street" is the avenue upon which the talented members of *NSync have always walked. But c'mon, a road with no bumps? It's like an *NSync song with no melody – impossible!

Believe it or not, these handsome hunks have had their share of tough days, hard knocks and, yes, even broken hearts on their way to stardom. And as one of the most down-to-earth pop bands to ever reach

such astronomical heights, the group will be the first to tell you: Growing up isn't easy, but it sure makes for one heck of a story.

Or, in this case, *five* stories.

So pull up a chair and get ready to get to know *NSync's members – Lance Bass, JC Chasez, Joey Fatone, Chris Kirkpatrick and Justin Timberlake – like you've never known them before. It's the guys of *NSync before they became worldwide performing stars.

And it all got started with a little twinkle ...

CHRIS KIRKPATRICK

Credit that twinkle to the eyes of one Beverly Eustice. It was she who gave birth to the first *NSync member-to-be – Christopher Alan Kirkpatrick – back in 1971. Of course, the new mom had no idea on that mid-October day in Clarion, Pa., that her little bundle of joy would eventually rock the world's stages with one of the most popular vocal acts in history. She just hoped he would learn to appreciate music.

There was little reason to think he wouldn't. After all, his grandmother was a trained opera singer; his grandfather was a country-western singer with five records under his over-sized belt buckle; his aunt sang in Pittsburgh jazz clubs; and Beverly taught voice lessons. Still, as normal as natural musical talent was in their family, baby Chris' abilities not only surprised mom, they actually scared her.

The story goes like this: The little toddler liked "Conventry Carol," a tune momma would sing to him often, but since he wasn't quite old enough to speak, Chris had to content himself with baby-toe

CHRIS KIRKPATRICK IN THE EIGHTH GRADE IN 1986 (BELOW) AND THE NINTH GRADE IN 1987 (RIGHT) IN DALTON, OHIO

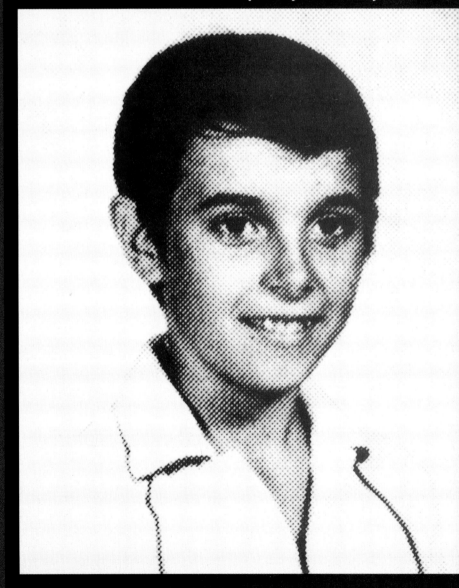

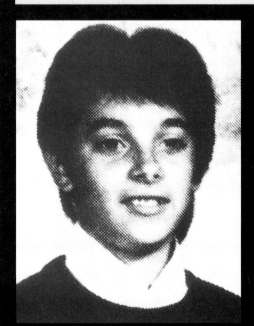

JOEY FATONE IN A SCHOOL PLAY AND AT HIS PROM IN 1995 (UPPER LEFT AND RIGHT), AND IN HIS SENIOR PHOTO (BOTTOM)

set out to carve his own niche wherever he went.

Chris became the class rebel, class clown and all-around trouble-maker. Of course, fans know now that his goofy gags and spectacular showmanship make him a perfect candidate for the limelight, but it wasn't until he landed the lead role in a school production of "Oliver" that others started believing what Chris already knew: He was destined for the stage.

A childhood spent dabbling in church musicals, school choirs and even football prepared Chris for the self-discipline and confidence it would take to succeed. By the time he graduated from high school, he was ready. Chris set out for Orlando, Fla., where he moved in with his father, Byron Kirkpatrick, and began taking acting classes at nearby Valencia College.

Still, he couldn't deny that his heart beat a steady tune for music. And a prestigious Orlando school, Rollins College, couldn't deny that tune was quite a captivating one! Chris earned a scholarship and made ends meet singing with pals in coffee shops, singing Christmas carols at theme parks, and eventually, by crooning along with the Hollywood Hightones, a doo-wop group that played at Universal Studios Florida.

Hearing himself sing "The Lion Sleeps Tonight" outside park restaurants wore thin after three years, however. At age 24, Chris wanted to move on. But how? He called his pal, Joey Fatone, another talented Universal Studios performer, and the two put their heads together ...

JOEY FATONE

As effective as the joining of Chris and Joey's heads was, it was nothing next to the pairing of their voices! As soon as the two started talking about putting together a vocal group, it became evident something super was about to happen.

tapping and gurgling. He apparently wasn't content for long. One day when mom passed by Chris' crib, she heard him repeating the tune, on-key (and no doubt, *NSync!) with the way she sang it.

Things only got weirder. When Chris was only 2, Beverly took him to see his first play, "Man of La Mancha." By time the pair arrived home, Chris had already memorized two of the songs. A genius? You bet.

An academic assessment test in second grade showed Chris was a "gifted" child. As a result, his elementary school pulled Chris from his normal class and put him into an accelerated one. That experience, plus family moves from Pennsylvania to Ohio to California, proved troubling. Separated from his friends and often having to make new ones, Chris said he often felt lonely, alienated and lost, so he

And why wouldn't it? After all, Joseph Anthony Fatone Jr. was on board, and he'd been flying – or at least trying to – since he was 8 years old! Yep, all it took was a small towel safety-pinned around his then-itty-bitty shoulders, a second-story window and the fearless attitude that has now become the friendly and flirtatious Joey's trademark. Although the Brooklyn bruiser eventually dumped the makeshift cape and window launch, the fearless attitude has certainly taken this Superman far.

Of course, a lot of trips to the hospital peppered Joey's road to stardom. Joey's dad even said the staff of the local emergency room knew Joey by his first name before the tot was 5. But on the rare times Joey's daring stunts didn't end in stitches, they typically ended in frenzied applause.

Joey loved performing. He remembers his first on-stage thrill – a kindergarten-age production of "Pinocchio" in which he played a small part – as the moment he wanted to spend his life on the stage. His mom remembers an even earlier performance: Joey, as a wee toddler, singing "Tequila" to his own

JUSTIN TIMBERLAKE IN THE EIGHTH GRADE IN MILLINGTON, TENN., IN 1995

JUSTIN TIMBERLAKE, THE WINNER OF HIS SCHOOL'S SPELLING BEE CHAMPIONSHIP IN 1995

mention work in another all-male harmony group, The Big Guys. Luckily, high school graduation and college-bound members broke this group up, and Joey's walk on the wild side as a singer and dancer with Universal Studios' Beetlejuice Graveyard Review kept him busy until that fateful day when he and Chris started laying the ground-work for their next dream: To reach the sky. All they needed was a little bounce ...

JUSTIN TIMBERLAKE

The boys found that bounce in Justin Randall Timberlake, already nicknamed "Bounce" for his love of basketball. At the time, the now-6-foot-tall cutie had just bounced back to his native Memphis, Tenn., from Orlando and was itching to make a career for himself either in the entertainment industry or on the NBA courts.

No doubt, fans are grateful that call from Chris rang through first! Still, even though that call was the springboard that would eventually launch Justin to fame as a musical performer, he had been taking leaps in that direction since he was only a baby.

Justin's mom used to say that he was like a little toy when he was a tot because she and his father would entertain themselves by playing fast music, then slow, then fast, while watching in amazement as their baby boy would keep time to the music with his little feet.

While that rhythm was natural, Justin's mom said that he probably inherited his voice from his father, a talented singer in a bluegrass band. Before he was 3 years old, Justin was able to harmonize with his father and songs he heard on the radio, she said. And since he was never without his favorite toy – a tiny plastic guitar – music seemed his natural path.

fantastic dance routine!

Was it the positive audience reaction or the heat of the spotlight that warmed this child's heart to entertainment? Ask family-man Joey and he'll tell you all that stuff's nice, but his true inspiration came directly from his father, a member during the '50s and '60s of a professional New York City vocal group called The Orions.

The elder Fatone instilled an appreciation for the arts in all of the Fatone children, and when it came time to bid Brooklyn good-bye during Joey's early teenage years,

the Dr. Phillips High School in Orlando, Fla., seemed a perfect fit.

The school's extensive performing arts curriculum shaped Joey's natural talents into professional-like skills, and quicker than Clark Kent can find a phone booth, the school promoted Joey to high-level chorus classes and granted him the role of Chino in the school's production of "West Side Story," both honors rare for newcomers.

But then again, Joey was special. A stream of musical-theater performances and small film and television roles followed, not to

Time spent in the church choir, singing lessons, school musicals and talent shows only solidified mom's suspicions, but it wasn't until he and some buddies mimicked the wildly popular New Kids On The Block for a school assembly that Justin's star quality shined as brilliantly as his voice. After the show at his own school and others, Justin and crew were chased down the school hallways by throngs of screaming female fans!

The Timberlakes had a hunch that Justin's star quality belonged on the syndicated TV series "Star Search," and the producers there agreed. At only 11 years old, Justin performed a country-and-western ditty to a television audience of millions. Though he didn't win top prize there, later on, producers for "The Mickey Mouse Club" picked him to be one of only 10 performers (among more than 30,000 kids) for the show.

At that point, Justin's life changed forever, not just because he learned the rigors of show business and honed his talents as a versatile performer, but because he made friends with a boy who would eventually become a key element in many of his future successes ...

JC CHASEZ

It may seem a little hard to believe that the same guy who now makes his living singing and dancing before thousands of fans – and who spent his teenage years doing the same for a television audience of millions – was considered extremely shy as a child.

Joshua Scott Chasez (only his mom calls him Josh) reserved his singing talents for family Christmas carols and showers and, instead, focused his energies on less solo pursuits like football and basketball, at which he excelled. It wasn't until he was 13 years old and a buddy of his dared him to get on stage and sing for a talent competition that JC took a chance on standing out and being noticed for his voice. Was it the dare or his buddy's promise of a $20 payday that got him up there? The only thing known for sure is this: JC brought the house down with a performance of Richard Marx's "Right Here Waiting."

That first-place win, along with a slew of others, gave JC quite a glow, but his mother was responsible for the push that really got the modest teen out of his shell. She had spotted

JOSHUA "JC" CHASEZ IN HIS FRESHMAN PHOTO AT BOWIE (MARYLAND) HIGH SCHOOL IN 1991

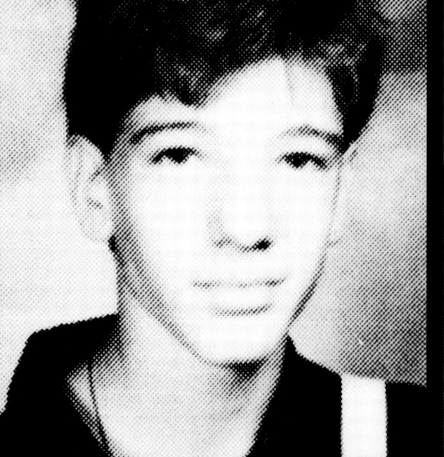

JC CHASEZ IN HIS "MICKEY MOUSE CLUB" DAYS

an open audition call for "The Mickey Mouse Club" and encouraged JC to vie for a spot. He might have dragged his feet on the way to the casting call, but once there, those very same feet got to dancing and absolutely wowed 'em. Ditto for that voice. In less than 10 minutes, JC had shown he was a star.

He maintained his spot in the MMC sky for four years, which he now says were some of the best of his life. Weekends spent on Florida's sunny beaches and weekdays spent with new pals, learning new dance moves and perfecting his already near-perfect voice made for what JC now calls a very affirming and positive teenage experience.

But even though JC carried a CD-sized claim to fame in his pocket when the show ended in 1994 – OK, it was actually a CD (JC was chosen to sing lead on the songs "I Saw Her First" and "Let's Get Together" on the club's MMC CD) – the still-modest talent moved right back to where he had always felt most comfortable: Out of the spotlight.

He moved to Los Angeles and then to Nashville, intent on learning all he could about engineering and production in the music industry. Little did JC know, his talent and knowledge only made him harder to forget. And his good buddy from MMC-days gone by, Justin, was one of the people upon whom he had made a lasting impression.

Justin made a call to JC not unlike the one he had received from Chris, and together, the four boys joined together and quickly got to work. Yet there was just one thing missing: That final link ... to make them all *NSync ...

LANCE BASS

Of all the guys, James Lance Bass will tell you he was the least prepared to make a career out of singing and dancing, but he was more ready than any of the bunch to hurtle skyward and work among stars. Of course, his celestial work had nothing to do with entertainment: Lance wanted to be an astronaut.

And the plan was already set in motion. As a child, math and science

were Lance's strengths. And as a seventh grader, the Clinton, Miss., native spent a week simulating Shuttle missions with NASA's elite at the Cape Kennedy, Fla., space camp. By the time Lance was finishing high school, he was class vice president and a National Honor Society member, and was also involved with Students Against Drunk Driving and the Fellowship of Christian Athletes. Clearly, college was on the map and space was still his final frontier.

But then fate intervened in the form of a local vocal coach. Not Lance's, mind you, but the singing teacher of some of Lance's closest buddies who, just by chance, had heard the teenager sing with a national touring group to which Lance belonged, the Mississippi Show Stoppers.

This vocal coach happened to work with Justin Timberlake, and

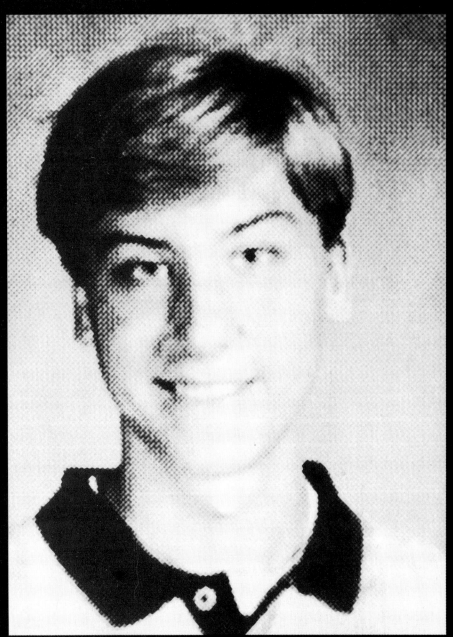

LANCE BASS DURING HIS DAYS AT CLINTON HIGH SCHOOL IN CLINTON, MISS.

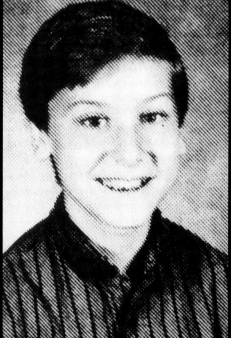

LANCE BASS AT A SCHOOL DANCE IN 1995 (LEFT) AND IN SEVENTH GRADE AT CLINTON JUNIOR HIGH IN 1992 (ABOVE)

when word got out that Justin and a few pals were looking for a talented and deep voice to complete their group, Lance's number was the only one worthy of being passed.

Of course, there was one small problem. Despite Lance's years in the church choir, the grammar school chorus and even the traveling Attaché chorus to which he belonged in junior high, Lance couldn't dance!

Or so he claims now. To hear the other members tell it, Lance was hardly ever a step behind, but the humble hottie swears he had two left feet. True or not, no one can deny that Lance put in long hours after the group's already-long rehearsals to practice the often complicated dance moves.

Obviously, his work, and the work of all the members, has paid off. They know it, the record stores know it, but most of all – and if you ask them, most importantly – their fans know it! *NSYNC*

MUST-KNOW *NSYNC INFO

*Think you know all there is to know about *NSync? Think again! Test your *NSync IQ and check out these 50 fun facts about your favorite musical sensation. Some of these might surprise you!*

1) Justin's mom Lynn came up with the group's name. It's an acronym featuring the last letter of each guy's first name (with a little cheating since Lance becomes Lansten – not his real name!). The breakdown: JustiN, ChriS, JoeY, LansteN, JC.

2) Speaking of names, here's what you'll find on the guys' birth certificates: James Lance Bass; Joshua Scott Chasez; Joseph Anthony Fatone Jr.; Christopher Alan Kirkpatrick; Justin Randall Timberlake.

3) Lance's favorite singer is country legend Garth Brooks. This is not too surprising considering Lance is actually a country boy himself (he was born in Mississippi). In fact, after Lance saw Garth perform in concert, he decided he wanted to be a performer, too.

4) On *NSync's first demo tape, the group covered the classic Beatles tune "We Can Work It Out."

5) Chris actually penned the lyrics to "Giddy Up," the show-stopping song that wraps up *NSync's debut U.S. album.

6) JC collects Hard Rock Cafe menus from all over the world, including ones from *NSync's overseas tour stops in Malaysia, England, France and Japan.

JOHN SPELLMAN / RETNA

JEFF SLOCUMB / OUTLINE

7) Lance recently had a guest-star role on an episode of the WB television drama "7th Heaven."

8) Justin does between 150 and 200 pushups each day. That must be how this man keeps his bod so buff!

9) The guys have two pre-show rituals. First, they toss around a hackey sack to get warmed up. Then they gather for a group prayer and hug with their super-close-knit posse of security guys and the road crew.

10) Before Lance officially joined the group and the guys became *NSync, there was actually another guy singing in his place. Unfortunately for him (and fortunately for Lance!), he could not commit to the long rehearsal hours and dedication the group needed, so he quit. (You know he's kickin' himself now!)

11) Although the group is based out of Orlando, Fla., none of the guys is a Florida native. Here's where they actually hail from:
Justin: Memphis, Tenn.
JC – Bowie, Md.
Chris – Clarion, Pa.
Lance – Laurel, Miss.
Joey – Brooklyn, N.Y.

12) Justin is the youngest and the tallest (6 feet) member of the group.

13) *NSync's first performance was at a showcase at Walt Disney World's Pleasure Island in October of 1995.

14) Joey has had small roles in two films, "Once Upon A Time In America" and "Matinee." He also guest-starred on the short-lived TV series "seaQuest DSV."

15) Joey and JC attended Dr. Phillips High School, a performing arts school in the Orlando area.

16) You probably won't see many slithering serpents in upcoming *NSync videos because JC and Justin hate snakes!

ANDREA RENAULT / GLOBE

17) Lance's favorite cartoon character is the Tasmanian devil.

18) Justin co-wrote the song "Good For You," which appears on the group's new album, "No Strings Attached."

19) JC has been moonlighting as a record producer. He produced the song "Fire," which he wrote for the all-girl group Wild Orchid. JC also sang on Blaque's hit song "Bring It All To Me."

20) Chris owns his own music and visual art production company, FuMan Skeeto, which has its own clothing line. And Lance's ex-girlfriend, "Boy Meets World" star Danielle Fishel, is FuMan Skeeto's spokesperson.

21) Justin founded the Justin Timberlake Foundation to improve art education in American schools. He even met with President Clinton and First Lady Hillary Rodham Clinton to promote his extraordinary efforts.

22) Check out these boys' battle wounds: Lance got the scar over his left eye in sixth grade, when he and his cousin were pretending to be American Gladiators. Joey got the scar on his left eyebrow when he hit his head on a light switch as a tot, and Justin actually broke a finger on stage once during their European tour.

23) Love Justin's curly locks? Well, get this: He used to HATE them so much that he wanted to get them straightened.

24) *NSync in ink: Justin, Lance, Joey and Chris all got the same tattoo during a visit to Toronto. The tattoo is of a fiery flame design.

25) Joey used to sport a silver hoop in one eyebrow, until "the powers that be" decided that wasn't cool for the squeaky-clean image they wanted the guys to project. Eventually, he let the hole close up, but did you ever notice that silly ski cap he wears in the "I Want You Back" video? That's to cover it up!

26) You know what they say about a guy's shoe size . . . here's how the guys measure

MUST-KNOW *NSYNC INFO

up: Chris – size 7, JC and Lance – size 11, Justin and Joey – size 12.

27) Justin loves Apple Jacks cereal.

28) Justin appeared on "Star Search" when he was only 11 years old.

29) Both Justin and JC strutted their stuff as members of "The Mickey Mouse Club." JC joined at age 13 and stayed on the show for four seasons, while Justin joined at age 12 and appeared for two seasons (along with fellow singing sensations Britney Spears and Christina Aguilera) until the show was canceled.

30) The group covered two songs on its first album: "Everything I Own" by the '70s group Bread and "Sailing" by '80s Grammy winner Christopher Cross.

31) The group formed in 1995, and Chris was the person who actually brought the guys together.

32) Was this boy bound for Broadway? In fifth grade, Joey played the lead in "Oliver," and his first stage performance was in the show "Oklahoma."

33) Chris is a HUGE football fan. He played it in junior high and high school and now he cheers on his fave home-state teams, the NFL's Pittsburgh Steelers and Penn State's Nittany Lions.

34) Justin starred in The Wonderful World of Disney feature "Janine and Alex: Cover Girls," which filmed in Toronto in 1999 and aired on ABC in March 2000.

35) Lance once toured with the United States' No. 1 show choir, the Mississippi Show Stoppers.

36) Joey had a childhood crush on actress Demi Moore.

37) JC's most popular character on "The Mickey Mouse Club" was Clarence "Wipeout" Adams, a hilarious dude with surfer attitude.

38) Lance is taking college correspondence courses from the University of Nebraska at

Lincoln (same as Britney Spears). His major? Business administration.

39) Remember *NSync's big break, the group's "In Concert" special for the Disney Channel? It was actually supposed to be the Backstreet Boys' big night, but that group backed out, paving the way for *NSync to skyrocket to superstar status.

40) Ever catch a glimpse of the Superman chain Joey sports, or the tattoo on his right ankle? It's because he's a freak for the Man of Steel. He collects tons of superhero memorabilia, including his fave – a vinyl Superman record album from the '60s. Joey even has been known to wear Superman T-shirts and jerseys on stage that had been given to him by fans only a few minutes earlier!

41) Lance and Chris are both afraid of heights, but both of them faced their fears to fly out over the screaming crowds during the song "Sailing" on *NSync's "Ain't No Stoppin' Us Now" tour.

42) The other guys nicknamed Lance "Scoop" or "Stealth" for the way this seemingly shy guy works the ladies.

43) Joey sang in "The Beetlejuice Graveyard Revue" at Universal Studios Florida. Maybe you caught him in his werewolf wear or vampire gear during a family vacation.

44) Chris loves to surf. Once (and we're definitely not recommending it), he even surfed off the Florida coast during a strong hurricane!

45) Chris is the only guy in the group with a college degree, an Associate of Arts.

46) Lance loves butter pecan ice cream, while Chris prefers Ben and Jerry's "Chubby Hubby."

47) Justin was elected president of his middle school's student council.

48) Joey's helping finance and create an acting handbook with his former acting coach, Karen Rugerio.

49) Chris also worked at Universal Studios Florida. He sang in an a cappella doo-wop group, The Hollywood Hightones, for more than three years.

50) Among the nicknames for Justin are "Mr. Smooth," "Baby," "Curly," "Shot" and "Bounce." ***NSYNC**

*NSYNC
LIVE

*NSYNC ALWAYS PUTS ON AN INCREDIBLE LIVE SHOW! CHECK OUT THIS SECTION OF NEVER-BEFORE-SEEN PHOTOS TAKEN BY FANS JUST LIKE YOU!

LIVE

JUSTIN AND CHRIS PERFORM FOR
FANS IN KALAMAZOO, MICHIGAN

LIVE

*NSYNC'S SHOWS ARE ALWAYS FULL OF SURPRISES, FROM THE 'MISSION IMPOSSIBLE' ENTRANCE (BACKGROUND PHOTO) TO SPECIAL STUFF LIKE 'THE BEE GEES MEDLEY!'

ALL THE GUYS IN *NSYNC GOT A KICK OUT OF THEIR 1970S OUTFITS ON THE "AIN'T NO STOPPIN' US NOW" TOUR.

LIVE

*NSYNC 73

BEFORE THEY HIT IT BIG, *NSYNC
PERFORMED AT THIS OUTDOOR SHOW
IN BURLINGTON, IOWA, IN 1998.

LIVE

LIVE

CHECK OUT THESE RARE PHOTOS FROM A FLORIDA 'NSYNC FAN ...

... THEY WERE TAKEN DURING 'NSYNC'S FAMOUS DISNEY CHANNEL SPECIAL!

LIVE

*NSYNC ALWAYS KNOWS HOW TO FIRE UP THEIR FANS.

THE MEN OF *NSYNC GET UP CLOSE AND PERSONAL WITH FRONT-ROW FANS.

*NSYNC Discography

Even the most devoted *NSYNC fan would have a tough time collecting every disc the group has released. In the United States, the group has put out three full-length CDs and only a couple singles. In other countries, however, the *NSYNC CD collection is more vast, with a variety of singles and remixes (with bonus tracks) and different full-length CDs. Expect to shell out a lot of cash at online music sites if you must have every *NSYNC release!

The following list does not include CDs for which *NSYNC contributed only one song, such as movie soundtracks (like "Tarzan") and compilations (like "MTV's Party To Go").

FULL-LENGTH CDs

SELF-TITLED DEBUT ALBUM (EUROPE, 1997)

Tearin' Up My Heart
You Got It
Sailing
Crazy For You
Riddle
For The Girl Who Has Everything
I Need Love
Giddy Up
Here We Go
Best Of My Life
More Than A Feeling
I Want You Back
Together Again
Forever Young

SELF-TITLED DEBUT ALBUM (USA, 1998)

Tearin' Up My Heart
I Just Wanna Be With You
Here We Go
For The Girl Who Has Everything
God Must Have Spent A Little More Time On You
You Got It
I Need Love
I Want You Back
Everything I Own
I Drive Myself Crazy
Crazy For You
Sailing
Giddy Up

HOME FOR CHRISTMAS (USA, 1998)

Home For Christmas
Under My Tree
I Never Knew The Meaning Of Christmas
Merry Christmas, Happy Holidays
The Christmas Song (Chestnuts Roasting On An Open Fire)
I Guess It's Christmas Time
All I Want Is You This Christmas
The First Noel
In Love On Christmas
It's Christmas
O Holy Night (A Cappella)
Love's In Our Hearts On Christmas Day
The Only Gift
Kiss Me At Midnight

THE WINTER ALBUM (EUROPE, 1998)

U Drive Me Crazy
God Must Have Spent A Little More Time On You
Thinking Of You
Everything I Own
I Just Wanna Be With You
Family Affair
Kiss Me At Midnight
Merry Christmas, Happy Holidays
All I Want Is You This Christmas
Under My Tree
Love's In Our Hearts On Christmas Day
In Love On Christmas
The First Noel

NO STRINGS ATTACHED (WORLDWIDE, MARCH 21, 2000)

Song list includes:
Bye, Bye, Bye
It's Gonna Be Me
This I Promise You
No Strings Attached
That's When I'll Stop Loving You
Space Cowboy
Just Got Paid
Good For You
Makes Me Ill
Digital Get Down

CD SINGLES (USA)

God Must Have Spent A Little More Time On You
Music Of My Heart (with Gloria Estefan)

CD SINGLES (EUROPE)

For The Girl Who Has Everything (includes "The Lion Sleeps Tonight," a previously unreleased bonus track)
Tearin' Up My Heart
I Want You Back
Thinking Of You
Together Again (includes "Sundreams," a previously unreleased bonus track)
U Drive Me Crazy
Bye, Bye, Bye